MW00769485

Island Child
— LBI —
Life Lessons from the Shore

Corinne G. Ruff
Illustrated by Lisa M. Benjamin

With contributions by Island Children of all ages

DOWN
THE
SHORE
PUBLISHING
West Creek, N.J.

The words "Down The Shore" and the Down The Shore Publishing logo
are registered U.S. Trademarks.

For information, address:
Down The Shore Publishing Corp., Box 100, West Creek, NJ 08092
www.down-the-shore.com

Printed in China.
10 9 8 7 6 5 4 3 2 1

Book design by Leslee Ganss.

Library of Congress Cataloging-in-Publication Data

Ruff, Corinne G., 1970-
Island child, L.B.I. : life lessons from the shore / by Corinne G. Ruff ; illustrated by Lisa Benjamin. -- 1st ed.
    p. cm.
ISBN 978-1-59322-063-1
1. Experiential learning--New Jersey. I. Title.
BF318.5.R84 2012
646.7--dc23

                                2012015339

This book is dedicated to L.B.I.
and to all those
who walked her shore;
yesterday, today and evermore.

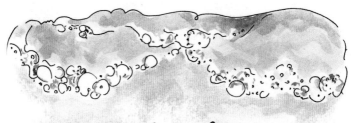

Foreword

Long Beach Island is a barrier island; in its most basic form it is a sand accumulation formed by the dynamic shifts of tides, currents, wind and waves. Each grain of sand that we sink our toes into, mold into castles and scrub from our scalps after a long beach day originates from a distance — from eroding uplands and marine sediments shifting with winds and waves. The gravel, sand and silt move along the northeast and are deposited by webs of waterways that lace into the ocean.

The sandy barrier islands work double-duty by both creating and protecting the bay. Without Long Beach Island, outflows of rivers and ground water from the land would mix and disperse into the ocean.

The hugging arm of the Island holds tight that mix of fresh and salt water to create the bay. With its dense integration of beach grass roots, it stands guard against the brutality of storm surges and waves, protecting the delicate balance of bay and marsh that is a nursery for the fin and shellfish. Those very creatures that inspire many an Island Child would not exist without the physical presence of L.B.I.

Inspired by the mesmerizing effects of the waves, I spent long hours as a younger Island Child searching the horizon for the origin of each wave that seemed to suddenly pop ashore. This inspired me to focus my undergraduate studies on the environment.

This new knowledge brought fresh perspectives on this ecosystem and I continued my studies on the human elements of environment and community.

Each day I try to inspire people, and get no greater joy than observing an "ah-hah" moment in someone's eyes as they gain a new perspective of our island from something I said, did or wrote.

I like to say I am happily doing my part, from my sandy piece of heaven on earth, to try and save us from ourselves. Changing the world one pen stroke, one paddle, one word; one person at a time.

Understanding the purpose and function of our island leads to respecting the vulnerability of it: Nature is wild and unpredictable — even with the most sophisticated of technology we don't know what is beyond the horizon.

To honor this, I tread lightly on the sand and glide silently over the waters penetrating a deep love and understanding of the dynamic natural systems that I live only peripherally within.

We are lucky to live in or visit this dynamic place. Passive recreational opportunities take us for fleeting moments into the spaces occupied by creatures that much like the tides, ebb and flow in an eternal cycle.

This cycle rotates around a clock, regardless of time or temperature. In May when many people are opening up their homes for the season, the horseshoe crabs are emerging from their winter hibernation out in the ocean, moving inshore in a prehistoric march to spawn under the lunar tides of spring. During blazing hot August days when kids are chasing the ice cream man, the fiddler crabs are sunning themselves on a marsh at low tide. When those lucky enough to know that it is "better in September" are enjoying cooler temperatures and a sparse beach, the shore birds are heading south as the water fowl move in. During the silent, late winter snowfall seals are frolicking near the inlet. The more we understand the parallel cycle the more we can honor it and protect it.

I have been an Island Child since birth. I am a Pisces, and I have salt water running through my veins. The Island has been my home base for solitude, exploration and celebration my entire life.

The Island Child book celebrates L.B.I. through personal stories and poems. The life lessons the Island has taught each of these con- tributors reflects their love of the Island like the sunset on the bay.

Angela Contillo Andersen

SEA FOAM

White froth rolls onto the shore with the waves. It is made up of many small bubbles that are trapped in a film of oil. Some believe that when mermaids die, their souls become the sea foam that glistens on the shoreline.

— THE LESSON —

Believe in mystery. Let your mind wonder and ponder life's many secrets. Use your Island Child mind to explore, imagine and dream.

First Faith

I believed if I could float
on the shore's overcast
into the spray painted mist
whose edge was the passion
I had only observed in a sunken
note my own, in my skin's
inability to do anything
but glow
in a bronzed hue;
the year when tee-shirts were first
multicolored and bathing suits
pink. I believed
clusters of sand crabs would rise
out of the oily sand to sink back down
farther than the undertow.

D.C., age 21

7

Introduction

The brisk spring wind blew through her golden curls as her cerulean eyes lit up with love. With her tiny, sandy hand outstretched, those rosebud lips curled into a smile. As she squealed with the delight only a ten-month-old could deliver, my daughter gave me the first and most perfect gift I will ever receive from her — a tiny seashell.

On the beach that day, I knew she would forever be an Island Child.

The name "Island Child" describes those who have a special connection to Long Beach Island, N.J. They are people of all ages who live on or visit this island. Their spirit is defined by their sense of adventure and wonder. They are as intrinsic to the beaches as the sand they stand upon. Their wishes are made on the moon over the ocean. Their smiles come from the sunsets. Their peace comes from watching the sunrise. The bay invites introspection and the ocean gives them strength. They are passionate about going for a walk on the beach. They know the perfect gift to give is a seashell.

The Island in this book is not exotic Bora Bora or glamorous St. Thomas, but Long Beach Island — a little piece of paradise for those of us lucky enough to have discovered her shores. Filled with natural beauty and character, this 18-mile-long island nestles up against the New Jersey coast, home to other beaches and islands that also inspire and nurture their "children".

On the north end of Long Beach Island sits a majestic lighthouse. When my son was three, I asked him what he thought the lighthouse was for; he replied "To light up the water so the fisherman could see the fish to catch them!" I described what its true purpose was and correlated it to a life lesson ("There are lighthouses in your life that surround you — God, your parents, grandparents, teachers, family, and good friends. They are your beacons of light that help you find your way when you cannot see clearly").

The special gifts of the Island — sea glass, the ocean, sandcastles, etc — and that conversation with my son, inspired me to write life lessons for my children about embracing individuality, developing strength, encouraging curiosity, cherishing family and friends. The Island Child concept took on a life of its own as more and more people were interested in sharing their own Island Child story — and so a book was born.

The elements of the Island draw people of all ages. As they reach the pinnacle of the causeway bridge, they let out a sigh of contentment as they gaze down on the Island stretched out before them. The summers are alive with the smell of fudge and suntan lotion, the laughter of children and the sight of the red and green traffic lights on the boulevard attempting to slow the fast-paced rhythm of the Island. The Island is bustling with energy as crowds of people vie for a spot on the beach or take to the bay in a boat. The winters bring cold, desolate nights as the traffic lights slowly pulsate their lonely yellow light, and the Island takes on a more natural state as the pace slows.

This island has inspired me my entire life. Both of my grandmothers loved the sea — the Island grounded and inspired them, and their families that followed. My gift is a heart that pulses to the rhythm of the sea. All they loved about the Island, I see. Even though they have passed on, I can still share the beauty that they saw: It is their gift to me, this island heritage — a cherished gift of love that I now share with my Island Children.

Come with us on a journey as the "Island Child" stories are woven in with life lessons learned from this inspiring island.

Corinne Gray Ruff

ANCHOR

A large hook cast overboard which secures a boat in place. It prevents the boat from drifting with the currents and tides.

~ THE LESSON ~

Let life's tides rise and fall around you. Let the waves of life's uncertainties crash upon you. Focus on what truly matters. Remain calm and secure: no storm lasts forever.

A life lesson I learned from the Island is that you need friends to help you get by things in life.   *L.M., age 12*

Living on the Island I have learned many things: How to get out of a rip current, how to fish, how to rescue people in the ocean, how to drive a motor boat. All of these things are very important to know while I live on the Island.   *C.B., age 12*

I was four years old when my parents purchased a summer home in Villas, New Jersey. I spent every summer of my childhood on the beaches of the Delaware Bay and my adolescence on the shores of the Atlantic in the Wildwoods. My education pulled me away from the shore and to the Midwest. I became familiar with the shores of the Great Lakes but nothing compared to the ocean. Every trip home was sweeter than the last. The ocean, the sound of the waves and the smell was life-renewing. You know "that smell"— the smell at sunrise just before you take the boat out fishing, or just after a thunderstorm or during a "stolen day of summer" in the fall. I met my husband during my time in the Midwest. Karma is strange. (What are the odds that I would meet a man from Long Beach Island in Chicago?). I was apprehensive visiting Long Beach Island. How could my ocean compare with another ocean? It could not be the same, there could be no substitute. And there was no substitute; the walk to the ocean in Long Beach Island was cloudy, overcast and windy (of course) on that spring day. The ocean was rough, the waves were beautiful, the dunes were amazing. There it was, "that smell," the aroma was like heaven. Every anxiety and concern melted away. I realized that is was all going to be fine. I had a new love and a new ocean to love with it. Life is good.   *D.K.L., age 42*

BOAT

A vessel designed to float on water.
Each boat has its own purpose:
sailboat, motorboat, speedboat, tugboat,
fishing boat, scallop boat, clamming boat.

——— THE LESSON ———

You and all that you are have a purpose.
Find it. Define it. Live it.

It was August 1969 and I was 13. My girlfriend Babe had a rowboat named Cecil, with an outboard motor. She and I would putter way out into Barnegat Bay at lunchtime armed with crackers, cocktail sauce and a clam knife. Overboard we'd go with our toes squiggling through the sand feeling for treasure for our lunch. Our feet would find about 20 clams and our hands would quickly toss 'em into the boat.

Suddenly my friend would scream in her high-pitched voice, "Oh no, here comes the Marine Police!"

As we didn't have a license to clam, we would toss our booty out of the boat. We would climb back into the boat with big, sweet smiles, waving innocently to two guys in a small police boat just doing their job. After they passed we'd spring into the bay, head first, eyes closed, searching the soft muck for our delectable stash. We'd bring 'em back on board, and the cracking, crunching nosh would begin.

P.T.C., age 54

Our family first discovered LBI in 1928 when my grandfather and grandmother lived on a large "wooden" boat at Gaskell's Marina (now Howard's Restaurant). Every year they would make the long boat ride from the Delaware River in Philadelphia to Barnegat Bay to spend their summers. After battling mosquitoes and green head flies, my grandmother put her foot down and a summer cottage was purchased. Now looking back over those years and our summer pictures, I realize that my grandchildren are the fifth generation to summer here and to boat and water-ski on the same bay. We would never dream of spending the summer months anywhere else. There is definitely a "Lure of Long Beach Island".

A.K.L., age 64

BRIDGE

Provides a way to get over a physical obstacle, usually land or water. It allows you to get from one place to another.

——— THE LESSON ———

Your attitude is your bridge to get over a mental obstacle. Think positive thoughts, have a great attitude and you will get over it.

Beginning at age nine I was lucky enough to spend summers on the Island with my parents and two brothers, family and friends that visited each year. Through the Island's resources and many friends I learned to enjoy fishing, clamming, crabbing, swimming and boating—all of which I still love to do today. The greatest thing that happened to me on the Island was meeting my wife, a vacationer on the Island. After forty-five years of marriage, four children and six grandchildren, we all still enjoy all that the Island has to offer. I guess it is safe to say that our whole family is "Island Children"—the Island is our natural heritage. My mother was the classic Island Child—she did not cross the bridge until after Labor Day. She walked the beach every day. Watching her and how much she loved the beach and the friends she made there is one of my most favorite Island memories.

R.M.G., age 68

My husband first introduced me to the Island twenty years ago, and I have since returned every year. It was the beauty and peacefulness of the Island that captured my heart, the changing colors of the marsh grass, and the way the light seemed to change each passing week.

My children have grown up summering on Long Beach Island. It is here where we seek peace and a relaxed life style. The Island is where I sought refuge after my cancer diagnosis, and also where I found the strength to face treatment.

A friend's mother once said we should leave all our "problems" on the other side of the bridge, and pick them up on your way home. Life seems to be happier once we cross the bridge. We are children of the Island.

R.D., age 47

Since I first went over the causeway my entire life has revolved around this island whether I have been able to be here or not. It has determined my every step, friendships, jobs, relationships, and even divorce when my devotion got to be too much for my ex-husband. (I believe the ongoing argument from my husband regarding our weekend treks was "I love Chinese food too but I don't need to have it every day.") We were married on the beach in front of my family house and we raced with our newborn daughter down to that beach in her first 48 hours of life. She is an Island Child.

The Island is my only constant. It is where my heart is. I cherish everything about it. When I am not on the Island I am truly a fish out of water. When I have been on other beaches in my travels I have been happy but I have not been home.

I will spend the rest of my life here, within the year I will be back year round. *S.L.K., age 55*

From the time I was born, my summers were spent at our Sears bungalow in Beach Haven Crest. The house, unchanged, still stands. Although no longer in our family, it will always be special to me. For it was there, I became an Island Child. Driving across the causeway, late at night, in jammies with the causeway lights flickering, my father would say "put down your window and take a deep breath…smell the wonderful bay air." But it wasn't until I heard the crunching of the driveway stones that I knew I was home. Walking barefoot in my jammies to the A&W for ice cream, fishing and crabbing behind the Acme, Lucy Evelyn, bumper cars and trampolines

at Hartman's, chasing the mosquito man, running on the jetties, beach bonfires...wonderful childhood memories. Now in Ship Bottom, I cross the causeway and drive right back to my childhood. I am an Island Child.

N.J.C., age 53

I consider myself an Island Child because the Island has been a part of me before I was even born. My mother always told me that I was a quiet baby in the womb until my father drove onto the causeway bridge on their way to Ship Bottom. I would kick up a storm, letting my parents know I was at my favorite place. The Island means a lot more to me today, after losing both my parents before the age of twenty. It's the place I go to not only clear my mind, but to be closer to them.

J.K.L., age 44

Are we there yet? I see the causeway! Here it comes!

Okay...The radio is turned off, the windows all go down, and a car full of excited Island Children make their boisterous approach onto the Island! Screaming, hooting and hollering from the start of the bridge to the boulevard! The smells, the feel of the sea air, the visual of all the water towers, and the excitement of arriving transforms us all — young and old. Now, we can start our summer! We love LBI!!   *L.D.O.*

I'm an Island Child because when leaving L.B.I., my sunglasses can never hide the tears that fall while driving over the causeway.   *K.P., age 33*

As we drove over the rickety wooden bridge, I would tell my younger sisters that the three Billy Goats Gruff lived under the bridge. They would ask my mother to please make me stop! My father would say, "Roll down the windows and smell the salt air!" Just the excitement as we entered the Island gave

17

me butterflies in my stomach. I was a teenager when my dad discovered the Island, and I thought it was our own private paradise. Today I feel the same way about the Island. It seems like yesterday, even though I am now 72 years old.

T.M.H. age 72

We are Island Children. Both my husband and I have been coming to LBI for over 35 years. We spent our summers with our moms and siblings, while our fathers commuted on the weekends to be with us. His family was from New York, not a bad trip, mine from Pittsburgh, a wee bit longer for my dad. While working at Breezin'Up in 1996 we met and the rest, as they say, is history. We married in 2003. Now our two daughters and I spend our summers on LBI with my husband driving back and forth from Pittsburgh.   *D.A.*

Long Beach Island isn't the South Pacific's Bali Ha'i, but it's been a special place for many an Island Child, including me. Once you have wiggled your toes in sand and dipped the same in the ocean along this part of the Jersey shore, you feel the unmistakable lure of this friendly island with its lighthouse overlooking Barnegat Bay. The moonlit, sunbathed, sandpiper-ed, sea glass, shell-collected beaches sculpted by sparkling waves of rhythmic rolling blues. Your ears rush to the music. It's the magic crossing of a bridge, you "get back to where you once belonged".   *L.T.E., age 61*

One Week! Heartbreaking, but that is the trivial measure of time our family gets to enjoy you in a year. Thank you for continuing to ensure the shack still stands, slightly more weathered than the year before. It is a welcome sight as we end our four-hour journey and travel over the causeway into your salty serene breezes and the real world melts away. As the years go by, we lay our heads further and further up-island, as a teen in lively and energetic Ship Bottom and now in the calm, relaxed beauty of Loveladies. Each visit, you never fail to surprise us

with something new, and generously fulfill our year long craving for relaxation, exploration and adventure. Again, we leave you contented, our hands brimming with beach treasures, hearts full of bliss and amid plentiful cherished memories. We will be back next year for more, old friend, so save us our spot on the beach.

K.H., age 49

The windows rolled down, the air takes my hair and tosses it playfully about. It electrifies my lungs as I drive with anticipation over the causeway. My cares and worries swept away, my heart is inflated with hope and possibility. There is nowhere else that I am this free, for I am an Island Child.

V.G.P., age 42

I'm grateful to be an Island Child. We started coming down to LBI when the bridge was made of wooden planks. Some of the best days of my childhood were spent here. The island has brought our family closer together. We found happiness here. I shall always be an Island Child at heart.   *S.L.G.*

On LBI I fish, I surf, I run, I play, I relax... therefore, I AM... an ISLAND CHILD!

J.A.G., age 33

BULKHEAD

A structure built along a waterfront to keep the land seperate from the water. Its strength is tested during a storm as the water crashes and pounds it. Everyday it handles the tides and constant pressure of the water. Even on the most serene day, as calm water laps at it, an unseen strength is present.

··——— THE LESSON ———··

Devote time towards developing your strengths: Strong body, strong mind, strong family, strong friendships and strong faith.

20

My parents brought me to the Island when I was two months old. I fell off the bulkhead into Barnegat Bay when I was three, and by the end of the summer learned to swim. I wandered wherever my bare feet took me—across empty lots, double rows of high dunes, and empty beach. I learned to read the details of the natural world—the swirling pattern the wind created on the flat bay, the cumulus clouds that billowed over the mainland to the west, the wind that rose about one afternoon. I played at the edge of the ocean, was spun by the waves. My children started life here; my parents ended life here. Now I live on land an ancestor bought in 1884. When I'm not barefoot, I still have sand in my shoes.

M.T.B., age 75

If you are barefoot and walking on the docks, pick up your feet — don't sweep them on the wood or you will get a splinter.

D.A., age 12

We knew we weren't supposed to go past the dock on the bay beach. But the wreck was so easy to reach at low tide. My friend and I would wade out to the dilapidated shell of the boat. Lots of little crabs and minnows had made their home on the watery floor, but we'd climb on top of the rotted cabin and commandeer it. We'd play chicken with the tide, jumping ship just when we feared the water surrounding us had become too deep. We might have bent the rules sometimes, but the tide was non-negotiable.

D.M., age 42

CLAMMING

Out in the bay a lone clammer wears his booties and holds his floating basket. His goal: a basketful of clams. He walks along the bottom of the bay feeling for them with his feet. One step at a time, one foot in front of the other, he finds his clams. They call this treading. Eventually, he fills his basket. Goal complete.

— THE LESSON —

Setting and achieving goals takes time. Go one step at a time. Have short and long term goals. Keep treading— you will succeed.

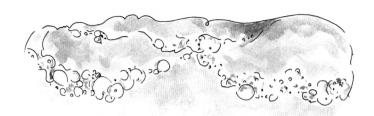

Growing up on Long Beach Island, it was always about the water. As a small child on the beach or in the bay, and as I grew taller and stronger working for my father at Houghton's Rowboats, every day—every waking minute it seems to me—was somehow connected to that God-like entity that ruled so much of my existence: Water.

Later, in my 20s, as I toiled in the clam beds out in Barnegat Bay, the water took on an even more vital aspect in my life. The money I gained from the bounties of that water helped me progress through college and into my career as piano teacher and mentor to many who want to learn the joys of playing and appreciating music.

Now, when I travel back to my ancestral home on Long Beach Island, it is so easy to forget what brought me to this point in my life. It is so easy to take for granted the water and the waves, and the true meaning of life and the many blessings I have received. I take this time to remember, and to always try to remember. And, to be thankful.

E.H., age 48

Walking in water has taught me to take one step at a time and to try my best. To reach the floating point you have to take one step into the ocean and keep trying until you get there. It taught me to keep going until I get there and never give up.

E.M., age 12

FISHERMEN

They are responsible for bringing in
their catch — A fisherman would
never take credit for a fish he
did not catch.

"— THE LESSON —"

In life, we must gently cast out
our own line to see what is out
there for each one of us. Each person
is responsible for creating his or her
own successes.

My Grandfather brought the dismantled carriage house from the west side of the state in 1926, then reassembled it on 11th St in Surf City. The up-and-down two rooms, plus privy out back, were a summer retreat until 1950, when heat and indoor facilities were added for year round living. We attended the just-opened school in Ship Bottom. Today's kids could not tolerate  the swarms of mosquitoes, but they would delight in the hundreds of half-inch baby toads hatching all over the Island in August. Catching and tickling blowfish in the clean bay waters without an adult in sight was not a worry for the grown-ups in those safe years. The sound of cars rumbling over the wood trestle bridges lulled us to sleep faster than an iPod or DS game would today. I remember the quiet. Sometimes the low voice of waves on the shore at night makes those halcyon memories fresh again today.

C.F., age 68

Waking just before the 1948 summer sun rose over the ocean at Spray Beach, I grabbed a bucket and tiptoed out of our apartment just behind the dunes, my feet sinking into the cold, damp sand, and climbed the dewy lifeguard stand, where I waited for Jo Ellen Lee, my very best friend that summer. She always came from 28th St. a few minutes late. We sat there in our sweaters, and didn't move before the first sliver of sun appeared; and then set out south on our daily adventure along the water's edge. Picking up only the best periwinkles and special shells, we aimed to arrive at our destination just before the pound fishing boats landed on the beach —just as the logs were thrown down in front of the boats to help the half-dozen fishermen, as they pulled on their oars and drove through the breakers up onto the hard sand. Dogs were barking, buckets clanging, fisherman throwing and sorting — below-minimum size fish here, valuable catch there. We selected some rejects for our buckets and trudged back north, the ocean now sparkling, our shells and fish sloshing together. Using the filleting skills of 10 year olds, we proudly presented our purloined booty for our mothers' skillets.

F.F., age 74

You earned your movie money and ice cream money for A&W by clamming with a peach basket in an inner tube at low tide. And you took your net to grab the shedder crabs. The locals never bought bait! They knew what tide to fish, how to rig for fluke and a few squid left behind by tourists and some live Kelly minnows you got with a net or bait trap was all you needed to get the fluke. You used wheel weights you melted down in a jig you bought from Bruce and Pat's.... We left out in the mornings too excited to eat! It was surf fishing a.m., crabbing or fluke in the midday, and surf fishing at dusk. A bamboo rod, a Long Beach reel and a rail road kerosene lantern were replaced as we reached the 1970s with a Coleman gas lantern with a mantle, a graphite rod, and Penn 750 spinning reels with Stren line! Oh it was heaven on earth!

W.J.M., age 53

I love the Island because I like to seine and fish a lot in the summer and there is a lot of water around the Island.   *D.D., age 7*

I am an Island Child, the ocean is in my blood, the sand is in my bones.   J.D., age 14

One thing I have learned growing up on the Island is once you catch your first white marlin you have to jump off the boat. The boat I jumped off was called the Mollie K. When I was reeling the fish in, I was so excited. The place I caught the fish was the Hudson Canyon. This is my experience on the Island. But there are many more for every person!   *J.T.*

Watching winters pass, summers come; but always feeling that LBI is mine. I remember catching my first fish from the ocean's waters. Tarnished fishing pole in hand, feet planted firmly on the sandy shore of LBI. My two-year-old self, grinning from ear to ear, despite the frigid December weather. I am an Island Child.
                    A.S.R., age 13

Growing up in Barnegat Light I always had something to do. Me and my friends would play at the lighthouse or at the docks, between the stacks of lobster pots left out to dry. As a son of a commercial fisherman me and my brothers would help my father unload the fish he caught almost every day. I fished with my dad in the summers and on weekends during school. I started running my first boat when I was 17 years old. I am still fishing (the *Viking Rose*) and loving every day.

                    T.B.

FOOTPRINTS

As you walk along the shore,
each step leaves an imprint of your
foot in the sand.

— THE LESSON —

You will walk many places in your life.
Look at your footprints. They remind
you that you are here NOW. You
are present. Turn and look behind you—
you have made your mark. Look ahead—
miles of empty sand; a place for you
to make an impression.

I was an Island Child long before I was born. My Mom and Dad not only share a love for Long Beach Island, they also became engaged listening to the crashing waves and were married at the Pearl St. Pavilion, feet planted in the sand. You can see how it is such a special part of me! I made my first trip to "Our Paradise" in Beach Haven at two months old, and I was happy as a "Little Barnegat Clam!" Each time our family crosses the causeway, we feel a little flutter in our hearts! My Mom and Dad can't wait to watch me grow and leave my tiny footprints on Long Beach Island.

L.C., age 1

Growing up on the Island, the lessons I have learned, and continue to learn from the beach, are too numerous to count. Nonetheless, they have molded themselves into my everyday life, be it on the Island or away at college, like footprints in the sand. The beach has always been my greatest constant in life— from beach walks in my stroller as a baby, to splashing in the waves as a toddler, to playing in the "hot sand" as a young girl; and finally to enjoying the simplicity of the sand underneath my back and the beauty of the crashing waves as a teenager. Lying on the beach day after day, the waves have taught me the most important lesson of all. Like the ocean waves that come in with the tides, but inevitably get pulled back out, my life resembles the sea. I will always come crashing down on this beautiful island I am fortunate enough to call my home, my haven. To me, the Island is the sand beneath the waves- soft and comfortable, here to break my fall, and worn with layers of experiences and memories that continue to grow.

N.A., age 19

I have been coming to the Island for over thirty-five years,
The beach has been my friend who's shared laughter and tears,

The times together are unlike any other that I've ever known,
It's the magical place where I've always felt like home!
Life's lessons were taught to me as I made footprints along the way,
How to appreciate family and health and not take for granted one day,
To enjoy daily the sun, sand, ocean and plenty of the fresh salty air,
And to also keep my life simple, focus, and try not to have a care!
Sunrises and sunsets are awesome—like a painting every time,
So glad I've had this spectacular island to always call mine,
For it's a surreal place that I've known right from the start,
For the rest of my life it will be in my soul and my heart!

D.S., age 55

I walked confidently and independently on the Island's beach sand when I was 11 months old, but cried and recoiled whenever my feet touched the grass. I am an Island Child.

J.B.H., age 3

Be it from far away or just the mainland, I always return to sit on the beach, wiggle my toes in the sand, gaze out at the waves, the ocean, the gulls, and feel every bit of stress drain from my body. It is then that I most appreciate the blessing that it is to live on this Island.

J.A.K.

I love the Island because it teaches you lessons and YOU'RE AT THE BEACH! *J.L., age 12*

I am an Island Child for my love of the Island, nature and swimming.
L.R.S., age 12

We discovered beautiful LBI when I was 12 (38 years ago!) and my family fell in love. Soon after, my parents, aunt and uncle and grandmother pooled their resources and bought a small house that we shared for many years. As a teenager, I dreamed of being able to spend my summers on LBI, but we had to rent out the house, so all year long, we waited for those last two weeks of August, Easter (sunrise mass on the beach), and Memorial Day weekend. Sadly, my family had to sell the house 10 years ago, but the memories of my children, playing with their grandparents, cousins, great grandmother, and great uncle stayed with me... as did the longing for my own LBI house.

Eight years ago, my husband and I bought our dream house, a little 50-year old bayside cape that needed a lot of love! I hope my children, who spent their teenage years living and working each summer on LBI feel as blessed as I have been, to be here with them, away from my classroom responsibilities for ten salty, precious weeks.

I am an Island Child because my dreams always lead me here.

L.W., age 50

I have grown up on this island my whole life.

G.A, age 12

HORIZON

The place at which the sea or land
meets the sky. From the shore, it
appears as though the ocean ends.
There is much more in the distance
that you cannot see; if you moved
towards this ending, you would see
that it is the beginning of the
rest of the world.

— THE LESSON —

Sometimes things appear to be ending,
but they are just beginning. There is
always something to look forward to
around the corner; there are things
that you cannot see unless you seek
to find them.

32

All right. I admit it. I'm addicted to Long Beach Island. Even the wicked Icelandic winters when the wind comes off the bay 40 mph; the soggy so-foggy-I-can't-see-the-road springs when the rest of the world is exploding in sunshine and flowers; the achey, stark lonely falls; the snarly touristy traffic-clogged summers. Even the greenheads. Even the mosquitoes. The turning

lane that nobody uses correctly; the dearth of restaurants open in the off-season; the pink, green, aqua, purple crazy quilt of houses; the Ferris wheel flashing in the center of town; the build-on-every-square inch zoning plan. Even the northeasters and flooded streets; the shack that no one will save; the way everything rusts. Even the houses that get knocked down. Oh, the beautiful, awful touching flaws of this place. Mix them together with Long Beach Island's out-to-sea simplicity and raw natural wonder, and you have a reality that's so compelling that I came here as a one year old baby and could never stop coming back. Long Beach Island is everything — a wetland at low tide, a gray day with a surround of horizon, thick salty damp air and a killer sunset, pisser clams and Whalers and the smell of asphalt mixed with popcorn, bumper cars and the sound of migrating birds; my childhood, my now and my future. Long Beach Island: it's where, when I go over the bridge, my heart knows that I'm home.

S.G., age 52

We look forward to greeting the sunset each evening during our long-awaited vacation this year. We will sit by the bay with a glass of wine and if we're lucky someone in a nearby house will be playing Bob Marley, or perhaps the discreet bagpiper's music will echo gently in the wind...

It truly is a wonderful life!

D.C., age 59

ISLAND

An island is land surrounded by water. As a defined area, you can use landmarks to get a good sense of direction. The sun rises in the east over the ocean and sets in the west over the bay. North is where the lighthouse is and to the south is the bird sanctuary.
The island itself is a compass.

·——THE LESSON——·

When you are lost, to get your bearings back you have to look at what is around you. Once you find where you are, you can plan how to get where you are going. In each of our lives, we are constantly making corrections to get to where we want to go.

Being an Island Child does not just mean going to the beach. To me, being an Island Child means feeling truly at home on the Island, which is exactly what it has become to me. It's a place to escape the real world for a few days and spend time with family. It's especially favored by my family and me in the winter when it feels like we are the only people there.

B.E.M., age 15

You know you are an Island Child when you have more toes on your feet than children graduating from your elementary school. You know you are an Island Child when your prom date picks you up at the yacht club after taking pictures at your home — a sailboat. I knew I was an Island Child when my pod of friends got bigger in the winter.

E.H., age 52

I am an Island Child because when I am here, I am at peace with myself and I am at my happiest.   *C.K., age 74*

I'm an Island Child because I live on a wonderful, exciting, safe 18-mile-long island. My island is special. In the winter my island feels like a remote island, but in the summer my island is crawling with people. I love being an Island Child. I believe it has many advantages and opportunities. I have a beach right down the street. My island never gets too hot, the salty wind is always howling. I'm so glad I'm lucky enough to be on an island.   *A.L., age 12*

I am an Island Child because I feel like I am a part of the Island.

G.A.C., age 11

We learn to stick together on Long Beach Island. My mommy and daddy would help any of the kids on our island and all of the other mommies and daddies would help me — if I needed help. We are a small group here, but, everyone really has each other's back. It is such a special place to be!!

Also, anytime you run into someone you know on the Island it is like a little party.

E.C., age 7

The Island has taught me to always be prepared for the west wind at the beach. When you're not prepared, the greenheads will bite you over and over. Greenheads are horrible at the beach, there are hundreds. They bite especially hard if you have salt water all over your body. This was a very annoying lesson to learn. This is my 6th year on the Island and I just learned this lesson two years ago.

A.R.M., age 11

I have been an Island Child my entire life. Summer vacations started with two weeks on the Island every June. Great memories of climbing the lifeguard stands in the evening, walking the Boulevard as a teen, and eventually bringing my own children to share the wonders of the beach. My life lesson from the Island is that time passes, but not on the Island. The sand is silky, the shells and sea glass lay waiting to be collected, the stars are always amazing and the power and wonder of the ocean all lie in wait for the next generation to experience. It's timeless, ageless and always wonderful — Long Beach Island.

J.D., age 61

This special Island is a place where someone can leave keys on the front seat of a car with an open driver's side window. The Island is a place for family, and a place to make lifelong friends while playing in the sugar sand. In the quiet dusk, with gulls laughing, the Island is a place where it's easy to believe magic can happen. I am so glad the Island is a part of me.

A.C.L., age 42

At Lucille's Candies in Brant Beach, it may have said "OH FUDGE" in big brown letters on the roof, but the corner window showcased an antique taffy making machine that was a joy to watch. Playing pranks on the salt water taffy making staff was an island diversion that kept my siblings and I occupied for hours and out of our parents hair. A series of rollers stretched the taffy towards the wrapper. Once the taffy was cut and the wrapper twisted on, it dropped into a basket below. The inevitable slip-ups of the machine and the frenzied workers held our interest. In absence of that, we'd cry wolf and point and jump up and down to get the workers to come running; only to find that nothing was wrong. When something did go wrong they wouldn't trust us, so we'd laugh hysterically when "naked" taffy fell into the basket or the wrappers ripped and didn't cover the candy properly. Today that taffy machine sits idle, a relic of the past; but alive in our memories as we reminisce about the hours we spent with our faces pressed up against the glass of that popular island candy store.

L.A.Q., age 55

37

KITE

As the flier and the string support the flight, the steady sea breeze allows the kite to dance in the sky.

— THE LESSON —

Watch the aerial dance. The dynamic path that the kite takes in response to the air reminds us to be carefree. Dance with sheer happiness for the joy in your life. Allow yourself to be moved.

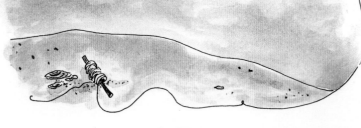

My family had always spent summer vacations on Long Beach Island. It was the only shore destination I knew. When I was ten, my parents took me to Atlantic City. I had never seen the bright lights or the boards. On the day we left Surf City to go to Atlantic City, I was thrilled. But that excitement turned to disappointment. Take me back to Long Beach Island. I wanted to create my own excitement: swimming, crabbing, and flying a kite. Fifty-five years later, I still feel the same. Long Beach Island is my only shore destination.

K.D.W., age 65

I love the Island because of the beautiful water and scenery, plus the bird and ocean life. Last but not least, the warm air and the warm water.

F.T.P., age 10

I am an Island Child because when I am here, my heart beats slower. I can hear it sing. Simply put, it calls me. I've learned that I have an inner artist. My inner voice is silenced with responsibilities of work, marriage and travel. Over the last five years, my ability to relax has dwindled. It's gone and I made a choice to find a way to save me. Here I relax, rest and take in the sea air. I can be. I am an Island infant. I have a retreat now to call my own in Surf City. My spirit is open to the Island's lessons. These lessons will also bless our children and grandchildren. It simply does not get any better — life at the beach, this beach.

D.M., age 55

I love my beautiful home by the beach.

S.K., age 5

LIGHTHOUSE

A tower with a beacon of light at the top that directs boats to safe harbor. The light also gives boats a fixed point to reference land. This light keeps boats out of danger, especially during times of bad visability.

— THE LESSON —

There are lighthouses in your life that surround you — God, your parents, grandparents, teachers, family and good friends. They are your beacons of light helping you find your way when you cannot see clearly.

My sisters and I have always had a very strong bond. Once, Nancy, my middle sister, and I were sketching down by the lighthouse in Barnegat Light. Nancy has MS and sometimes she cannot walk very well. We were enjoying our time together when a boat sailed past. Since, most boats have names, we were delighted when we saw this one was called TWO SISTERS.

Just a few moments later. Two seagulls landed close by. One of them only had one leg. We took some snapshots of both coincidences and always remember this day fondly!   *W.S.M., age 60*

I love the Island because of the ocean, and the beach. I also love the sushi, and ice cream shops. But my favorite things about the Island are the lighthouse, And the creatures that live in the ocean, and the bay.   *B.C.R., age 9*

My fondest memories are of my aunt and her friend, sitting along the edge of the ocean very late into a summer afternoon, with the waves at their feet, and large straw sun hats. My aunt has been gone for eleven years, but her spirit lingers on. As I sit on the 11th Street beach in Surf City, I can almost see them now. The sun hat is now in my home as a reminder of beautiful Long Beach Island days gone by. I was in love with the Lucy Evelyn. How I looked forward to visiting that wonderful old vessel. I was heartbroken when I learned of the fire that cold winter evening, which destroyed her. But we still have Old Barney. A trip to Long Beach Island is never complete without a trip to Barnegat Light or a burger at The Holiday Snack Bar. I have never missed a summer visiting Long Beach Island. There is a magical feeling that Island Children will recognize immediately when they cross the bridge.   *S.K., age 63*

I took my first steps on Long Beach Island. I still have the photos of me in my two piece bikini and all. Even then I knew there was nothing like the feeling of sand between my toes. I was lucky enough to spend every summer here.

My parents were original owners in High Bar Harbor. After I got married I moved to Long Beach Island year round. My three children all took their first steps on the same beaches of Barnegat Light that I did as a child. They even believed Ol' Barney was their personal lighthouse. I've moved across the causeway, but maintain my family's home for many summers to come. I know my grandchildren will one day be Island children of Long Beach Island. I proudly display my "Local" bumper stickers on my minivan.

M.M., age 40

My love for Long Beach Island began when I was a six-year-old child, and is as strong today as it was that first day many years ago. Barnegat Light beach, Andy's, the Islander, "Shrimp Basket" dinners at the Dutchman's, Kubel's, Gateway, Plantation. Fishing in the surf or on the Captain Bill—catching and eating the same day. Finding the "best" shells and sea glass. My husband and I now live on the mainland bayside, directly across from Barnegat Light. We have the unique pleasure every day and night to see Old Barney. The love goes on and is never ending.

D.P.G., age 59

Words and lessons that come to mind when I think of Long Beach Island are family. I have a very fond childhood memory of spending summers going "down the shore" to our grandma's house where we would love to visit our family and friends. I would love that feeling of excitement and contentment as we drove over the bridge and could smell that fresh salty air. I have an extra fond memory of spending July 4th at the beach when my grandma's neighbors would host the annual beach party. The horn would blow to signal the games followed by a cookout and a day filled with playing at the beach and then off to watch fireworks over the bay. I recently moved to a coastal town in Massachusetts with my husband and two beautiful children with hopes that they have that same connection to family and the shore as well.

J.M.H., age 34

The waves move my soul,
As they break upon shore.

The shells pursue the waves,
Until a human comes along to redeem it from the ocean.

The sand is, well... just there.
Nobody knows why, but they assume there is a reason.
I believe it is there for comfort and warmth.

Even beaches have mysteries too.
Like why the ocean has waves,
Why the fish swim,
And why we enjoy its vivid tranquil beauty.

These are questions even I do not know.
I'm not entirely sure why but I assume they are there for...

The beauty and life they fill the beach with.
But I do know why the ocean is my favorite place...
It's where I belong.

Once you step foot on its exquisite invite to paradise,
Everything that happened is gone.
Nothing is left in your mind but pure freedom.
There is nothing you can't do,
And nothing can bother you,
For I feel it's a blessing that lasts forever.

C.C., age 12

MOON

The moon shining on the water
is a magical sight. To shine, the moon
must reflect a greater light — the
light from the sun.

·⌐ THE LESSON ⌐·

It is during our own quiet reflection
that we gain our most brilliant ideas.

I have been an Island Child since 1967 when my mother and father built our home on the Oceanside in North Beach, Lane 17. This experience was life changing, and is stuck within me so deep, like gum you cannot remove from your shoe. I recall running on stones all summer till my feet were so tough and black that nothing could penetrate them; living in my bathing suit with salty skin all day and night because at any given time I might go back in the water to swim; being saved by the lifeguard because the undertow was so fierce, (it taught me to love and respect the ocean); walking on hot, white, sand that squeaks, digging for sand crabs and letting them tickle my hands; finding phosphorescence in the sand and thinking it was aliens. I remember Flamingo Golf, the Sand Bar ice cream, Old Barney, eating blue claw crabs—and the reflection of a full moon so bright, it is a staple in my reservoir of memories like none other. These are some of the reasons this island will never leave my soul.   *F.A., age 50*

I love the Island for its informal, easy way of living. I love the sunrises and the sunsets and the beautiful full moons. Many years ago, the long walks on the beach in the early morning and also combing the beach after a northeaster.   *J.S., age 87*

I always remember the peaceful times; the smell of the salt water and the waves crashing at night. My two daughters collected shells with their grandmother and sang songs as they walked along. "Surf Side 6 Margie" was the most interesting Island Child in Surf City for 92 years and someone everyone wanted to be with. This is what LBI memories are made of...   *P.G.*

OCEAN

A massive body of salt water covering the earth. Deep currents are created by differing amounts of salt and water temperature;
Shallow currents are created by wind—these highways in the sea are the result of uneven solar heating. The ocean's strength is defined by the currents not only within its depths, but all around the earth.

— THE LESSON —

The strength of good character is formed through trustworthiness, honesty and accountability.
Like the constant motion of the ocean, the unstable nature of life creates opportunity to forge good character. How well you positively affect other people reflects your strength of character.

46

What I love most about the sea is this; when I walk into the ocean I am entering a time machine. It feels, looks, and smells exactly the way it did when I was a child with my dad, a young girl surfing the waves, a teenager frolicking with friends and now a young mother bonding with her son. Everything in this world changes around us, we get older, architecture changes, restaurants and stores have new names, even people come and go in our lives. However, when I enter the ocean now in 2011, it could be 1976, 1985, 1992 it does not matter the ocean is exactly the way it was the first time I ever swam in it, it never changes. I can float and swim and in my mind I'm twelve years old the furthest one out, out by the buoy that used to be there. I'm any age I want to remember. Nowhere else other than my friend the ocean can give me that memory flashback so real, so spiritual, so inspirational.

B.G.P., age 38

I love the Island because it is beautiful. I am so close to the beach and it is not crowded. I have learned not to swim or eat ice cream without a buddy.   *D.V.L., age 10*

I am an Island Child because of how much I love beaches and bays.
K.L., age 12

I am an Island Child because I know my way around the whole island. I practically live on the beach and can't get enough of the water. I love the breeze in my hair.

D.D., age 12

I know I am an Island Child because the whole year through I live and enjoy the Island. I have seen everything on the Island that there is to see. I even remember the first time I went to the beach. I went in the water slowly and dove under each wave because I didn't want to get swept off my feet. My little brothers played in the sand. I still remember that day as if it were yesterday.   *A.M., age 11*

A lesson I learned from the Island is how to swim. I had to learn how to swim and be safe in the ocean. I took swimming lessons and learned what to do if I ever get stuck in a rip current. I was told not to panic and to swim parallel to the beach. Now I am not afraid to swim in the ocean.

L.T.P., age 12

I love the water. I live in the water. That is what I was born to do. If you try to move me to the middle of the country, I'll find my way back to the Island somehow. It's part of me. I don't know how to explain it. It just is. Even though I'm not the fastest swimmer in the world, I still live and breathe water.

M.G., age 12

I am an Island Child because I understand the peace and solitude and the activity of the Island. It is like an ocean wave; it builds up getting bigger and stronger and it will start to crash down, its water lapping at the shore. This is how I find life on Long Beach Island. It's a climax in a book. It gets more interesting until it's done. You must learn to live it.

C.M., age 12

I love riding the waves and getting ice cream from the ice cream truck.

L.S., age 4

There is no better smell to me than that of the ocean, while standing on the beach during a gentle east wind. It's a live, visceral smell; better than the most aromatic flower or candle.

D.K., age 39

Sometimes the water on the Island looks too rough to go in. But if you're strong enough to swim through the waves there's a calm sea on the other side. Life, like the ocean, can hit us with one crashing wave after another. We have to be strong enough to dive into our problems and swim past them. They won't go away if we just sit on the beach and stare. Then comes another lesson...once we're past the waves, we can't let the undertow created by previous problems pull us out toward sea. We have to fight against the current to maintain the peace we've found.

J.O., age 40

I'm an Island Child because when I swim in its water, it makes me feel like there's no better place.   *L.M., age, 9*

I am an Island Child because I live on an island. I like being an Island Child because most people don't get to live near the water and live on an island; most of the time I hang out at the beach and walk on the jetties to see what I can find.   *L.Y., age 12*

The ocean is my home, my summer getaway-place to live like a mermaid.   *A.Z., age 12*

Saturday mornings as a child, packing lunches, knowing that the Island was 90 minutes away. Car ride, anticipation, arrival.
Riding waves, frisbee, hoagies.
Sunset, sand in my pants, home.
These memories will be with me forever. It is our family's common ground, no matter how far we go. We come back to the Island every few years to reconnect with each other and those memories.

S.G.B., age 50

I'm an Island Child because of how much I love the water. I love swimming. You can do so many things with a body of water and an imagination.   *K.A.F., age 12*

SAILING

Wind across a sailboat's sails moves the boat along a path. The boat is an instrument, the sails are the notes, the wind is the tune and the path is the song. Sailing is a nautical symphony.

———— THE LESSON ————

In life you are given a blank piece of sheet music. Embrace your unique talents. Discover and believe in what makes YOUR heart SING. Self confidence is like the sails on the sailboat, you're not going anywhere without it. Be deliberate, stay the course and live your life's symphony.

50

I am an Island Child because my family has been coming to Long Beach Island since my great grandfather was forty-nine years old. I have been coming down here since I was two weeks old, so has my mom, and grandfather. I come to Long Beach Island every summer. I have learned so many things here, from my first steps to sailing different boats. Long Beach Island has

a very special place in my heart. I was born into the Island just like I was into my family. This Island is half of my life. It's like I live two very different lives: here in the summer in Harvey Cedars and my winter home. I love this Island because of the friends I've made and all the happy times.

T.C., age 11

Ever since my first year of living I lived on the Island. I'm an Island Child for so many reasons. I love the Island and enjoy finding surprises on it every day, whether it's sailing in 25 mph winds, water splashing on my face or surfing the giant wave rocketing toward the shore. My favorite time at the beach is after a hurricane strikes. The rough water and giant waves are always washing you back to sea. It's just a battle to get to two feet out, but it is a challenge I am happy to take.

S.T.B., age 12

I am an Island Child, a summer "immigrant" with Brant Beach memories from the '60s. During several teenage summers I fell in love, made out to the Beach Boys, learned to fish, enjoyed salty kisses, sailed a boat, and made new friends. And while I've been to many islands in the decades since, LBI dreams still fill my nights.

W.R., age 66

Summers on Long Beach Island were special to me. They gave me an opportunity to spend time with my grandparents and my cousins. My cousins and I clammed, sailed and water-skied in the bay and played on the Harvey Cedars'/Loveladies' beaches (without beach badges). My grandparents had one of the last remaining oceanside to bayside strips. As a result, we were able to carry the Hobicat across the boulevard to launch the boat into the ocean.

Whenever we stayed with my grandparents, whatever we caught we ate: clam fritters for breakfast and blue fish or blowfish for dinner. After harvesting mussels from the jetty, we would soak them in beer and then stream them. What a treat!

We woke every morning to the words, "Swimming! Swimming!" We were like lemmings going to the sea. Without taking the morning swim, you wouldn't even think of going to the breakfast table. Meals were fun—everyone sat at the large table eating and talking together.

D.D.

I will always consider myself an Island Child. My youth was spent at the beach in southern California. When my husband and I moved to the east coast fifteen years ago it was Long Beach Island that quickly became our weekend getaway from the Pennsylvania suburbs. My husband was an 80th street lifeguard during his college summers and surprisingly that's the same spot our family rides the waves now. I'm on Long Beach Island all summer with our three very active kids. I wake up to the sun with open windows, open curtains, birds chirping and bike all day to get the kids to swim or sail lessons and swim meets in Harvey Cedars. My four, eight and ten year old children are my joy in life and connection to my youth. I look at life through their eyes and reflect how I was at their age. At times I think I'm a teenager, how active I am with them. They keep me young at heart and spirit. So with our SPF 50 lathered on, the sun shining, and the sound of the bay in our ears, we are in search of another perfect Long Beach Island day. We look for sea glass, play paddle on the beach, listen for the cow bells alerting us to the ice-cream trucks or take a swim. This is our summer time together and we love every moment when we are on Long Beach Island.

K.S., age 46

Causeway lights, like a string of pearls, sadly signaled the end of summer, tears flowed.

When it began, it was an endless summer filled with possibilities and the smell of Coppertone.

"Get Down Tonight," "Island Girl," and "Jive Talkin'" blared from a transistor radio

Discovering the simple pleasures of beach glass and the Five & Dime decades before the cell phone

Now my daughter is an Island Child, too

I hope the simplicity of sunsets, rusty bikes, moonlight twinkles on the ocean, and sailing will be hers her whole life through.

L.V.S., age 52

SAND

Each grain of sand on a beach is special. Each grain has a story to tell about its origin and history. Each piece comes from a type of rock or mineral. It has traveled a long journey to be there among all the others — to be one of many.

·· —— THE LESSON —— ··

A grain of sand is an infinitesimal glimpse of You in the universe. Each of us has our individual story of origin and history. Together, we are all part of a very big picture.

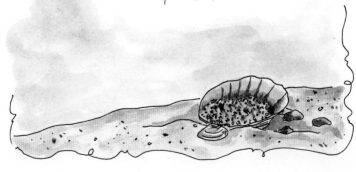

I became an Island Child when I brought my own children to Long Beach Island nearly forty years ago. I remember climbing over the dunes, my young daughter marching ahead with her bucket and shovel. I struggled with my son on my hip and various beach paraphernalia. I vowed when I reached the top of the dunes I would set him down. He would have to walk the rest of the way. When I did, he stood there saying, "Sand! Sand, Mommy, sand!" He said this over and over as he stood rooted to the spot. I still know that exact spot.

Now that I've written this, I just might go back there tomorrow!
                                                                                          P.T.E.

My favorite Island Child is the child I was in Harvey Cedars, before the summers of work began; when the long days blended into each other, and the only concern was the condition of the ocean — jelly fish? rip tide? Spending all day in the water until my lips were shriveled with salt and my shoulders just beginning to hint at the sunburn that would come, then finally flopping on a sandy towel to warm up under a sun that seemed to embrace everything. Staying in the outdoor shower so long we'd get yelled at for flooding the yard. I remember bonfires on the beach, and my salty-damp sweatshirt, and finally falling asleep, exhausted "from the salt air," in a bed that always contained a bit of sand.

Beach days were broken up by the occasional drive to the Lucy Evelyn or the lighthouse, or just mucking about on the bay, where the smells of creosote, marsh and boat engines were a world apart from the beach's offerings of Coppertone and salt spray.

Rainy days also brought change — a walk to the Ship's Wheel to get comic books, Pixie Stix or art supplies. I would wander the drizzly, empty beach, where the sand was sometimes still warm and dry under its wet, dented surface.

Sometimes now I'm too busy or distracted to conjure up that Child, but when I can get to the beach, I flop down on my towel, turn my head toward the sea and wait. I feel the grains of sand under my cheek, and suddenly I can see her there: tan and scrubbed by waves, her hair drying in salty tangles, intent on following the wrack line at the edge of the water. She pauses only to pick up a shell, or maybe a piece of sea glass, and then disappears down the beach.

L.G.

I am an Island Child. My best memories of growing up are on Long Beach Island. Though I didn't know it then, I met my future husband breakdancing at the clubs on Teen nights, hanging out at Fantasy Island, enjoying the adventure and the freedom of beautiful beaches and bustling boulevard. No matter where my life's adventures led me, I always longed for the comfort and sense of security that I get from this place. It feels like home. My husband and I said our vows here, on our beach pavilion, with sand in our shoes. Like the spice of life, the salt air leaves a film on everything we own, the sand is everywhere, in our car, in our bed. There is nowhere else in the world I would rather be raising our daughter than here on Long Beach Island with the beach as her backyard. My soul's rhythm is in sync with nature here, from the moon's pull over the ebb and flow of the tides, the awesome sunsets over the bay, even the changing seasons.

I still enjoy the peace and serenity of a walk on the beach in the middle of winter, bundled up beyond recognition of course to protect from the frigid wind. That's when beachcombing is the best. I am like the sea glass that I search for. I was tossed in, broken, jagged, and unfinished. The positive loving energy of nature I associate with this island has transformed me into a polished treasured jewel.

K.D., age 41

Sitting on the beach I watched my seven-year-old son dig a hole. No shovels, no buckets —j ust his hands. Sand is flying everywhere. He is getting sandy and wet two things, I repeatedly told him not to do but how can you not dig a hole on the beach?

But why? Why does even the most fastidious child find it absolutely fascinating to sit on the sandy shore and let little beads of broken rock and glass slip through his fingertips?

It is simple...treasure.

The treasure we seek isn't an old box filled with gold, it is in the sand, the waves, the air and the forests—everywhere at the shore. So dig away. I know I have found mine.

C.E.G., age 40

I came to the Island as a twenty-two year old adult and instantly regressed to the life of a child. I frolicked in the surf; built castles in the sand; and waited the required hour after eating before going back in the water. Now, as a much older adult, I love to frolic in the surf and build sculptures in the sand. And, because my mother is not here to enforce the rule, I don't wait an hour after eating before going back into the water. I am no longer a child, but will always remain an Island Child at heart.

C.B., age 69

My first visit to the Island was in 1970 when I was dating my husband, who was raised on the Island. While my children were growing up, I brought them to the Surf City bay beach almost every day. Just the feel of the sand walking over the dunes, smelling the salt air, feeling the ocean breeze on my face, and taking in the beauty of the ocean gives me such a feeling of serenity and peacefulness. I have so many wonderful memories of the Long Beach Island—times spent with family and friends.

D.L.E., age 60

SANDBAR

In a body of water, currents or waves create an area of accumulated sand. The result is a bar of sand hidden just below the surface of the water. The shallow water may cause a boat to run aground.

— THE LESSON —

No matter what your speed or direction, be on the lookout for hidden dangers. Prepare by knowing trouble spots exist and have a plan to navigate around them.

I am an Island Child because I love being really close to the water. I love the ocean with its crashing waves. It is fun to swim with the waves and to go boogie boarding. It is a lot of fun watching my Uncle Jonny surfing in the ocean, and it's also fun when he teaches me how to stand-up surf in the bay off Sunset Beach Park in Harvey Cedars. Going on my Gigi's and Paddy's boat in the bay is so awesome! Building sandcastles and towers is what I like to do on land. Playing in the tide pool and playing tag with my cousin, Jack, is the most fun ever.

B.W.P., age 7

My friend the ocean it crashes on the beach; it has high and low tides. It offers wonderful sandbars and blustery winter waves. Seagulls and other shore birds flock to it and so do we, the true friends of the ocean.

B.G.P.

I am a Jersey Girl! I have been coming to the Island since I was born in 1998. It is like my second home, and better than my first. Even as a thirteen year old, I already have so many amazing memories from Long Beach Island. First is the food: Rita's custard and Italian ice, pork roll egg and cheese sandwiches, hot and dirty crabs, Jersey rolls and Okie's steak sauce. I love mini golf with my family, the white fluffy sand and big crashing waves, and the shells and rocks that you can never find anywhere else, not to mention the Long Beach Island sunset you can't beat. You never have to get into a car on the Island; all you need is a rusty old bike to get around. Finally, my favorite of all is the scent of the warm Long Beach Island air that smells like pine trees and the ocean on a beautiful summer night.

G.N., age 13

SANDCASTLES

Sand artistry: beautiful creations
made from hands molding sand. As
the tide comes in, the castles are
washed away forever.

— THE LESSON —

As we create, we learn our capabilities.
This knowledge remains with us forever;
what we create sometimes does not.
Keep this perspective as you travel
through life.

I love Long Beach Island and I love the summer. The things that I love to do at the beach are playing in the sand, making sandcastles, going swimming in the ocean with my dad and playing run the bases (our game of baseball). I spend my summer here with my family. For eight weeks I'm on a swim team in Harvey Cedars. Last summer we came in second place. I love the swim meets. I take swimming and sailing lessons during the week. On the weekends we go to 80th street and watch my parents play volleyball. I have fun every day!

A.S., age 8

I am an Island Child because I like the sand and the water... I like running around sticking my feet in the water, and running away, and jumping in the water. I like playing with sandcastles and collecting sand in my buckets and then running away from the waves before they can get me. My uncle holds me on his surfboard in the bay and I get to surf, too. That's really fun.

A.N.P.

I love the beach, the seagulls, the water, the sand, and the ocean breezes. It is fun making sandcastles and swimming under waves, but my favorite part is making new friends.

B.M., age 6

Since I was a little girl, I have been visting LBI and in a nutshell it holds some of the best summer memories I have!

What I love about LBI is of course the sunny, warm days with my one-in-a-million family, the laughs we shared and the fun times we had year after year! I remember in particular the July 4th celebrations and all the fun activities packed into that day.

Now in my thirties, the good times continue with my own children. I am counting down the months until summer comes again.

T.W., age 40

SANDY FEET

Grainy sand adheres to your feet as you walk the beach. The true mark of an island child — proof that you were on the beach! A deep connection to the earth is felt as the sand hugs your feet. Each piece clinging, not wanting to say goodbye — much like a dear friend when the time comes to part.

—— THE LESSON ——

Stay connected. Allow yourself to be embraced by nature and those who surround you. HUG!

I'm an Island Child because I find wearing close toed shoes, or shoes for that matter, to be utterly suffocating.

S.P.

I love the Island because getting a little sand between your toes fixes everything.

M.L.P., age 29

I am an Island Child because I was born and raised here. I love to hear the sound of the ocean waves crashing and the sand seeping through my feet. I enjoying swimming and everything about the beach. There is so much to do no matter what time of year!

V.G.R., age 9

You have to love the Island with all your heart to never be annoyed by the sand in your shoes, house, hair, and everywhere, and I don't mind it at all.

M.L.F.

I am an Island Child because the sea salt smell and the rippling bay are my favorite things. I love the feeling of the sand between my toes and the squeaking of the sand as I run across it. There is no better feeling than the one you have after watching the sunset over the bay; so many colors but so small in a great space.

SEA GLASS

A tiny piece of glass was once a part of a whole glass object. The power of the ocean broke the glass into many fragments. The motion of the ocean sanded the jagged edges smooth. In time, the small pieces of glass wash upon the shoreline as smooth beautiful jewels from the sea.

THE LESSON

Time changes all things. Bad memories fade and good memories become even better. Time polishes the broken pieces of our hearts. Time makes the happy heart glisten.

Oh sea-glassing — what sweet memories. Strolling along barefoot with my husband and little ones with hopes of finding a treasure from the sea.

M.M.

Mom is an Island Child. I am an Island Child. I have Island Children. Winter is my favorite time to come "home." Sea glass is aplenty and the sound of the waves is all I hear on those crisp, vacant mornings on the beach. The first moments of each visit, I walk down to the beach and take a deep breath of that wonderful sea air. My teenage daughter says, "It smells like fish, Mom"—but it's perfect. It reminds me of all the times I've spent here —the funny memories, the stories from vacations past. I'm an Island Child.

K.M., age 37

I started coming to Long Beach Island as an infant. My grandmother bought her first house in Ship Bottom in 1922. Every summer we would travel from North Jersey the day school got out. We would spend our days on the beach and our nights chasing the mosquito truck. We headed home on Labor Day with wonderful memories. As the years went by I continued to come to the Island every summer. My daughters began to call it "their beach." My dad woke me every morning for a sea glass search on the beach. Dad always found more. Now that Dad is gone I have inherited the beach and am lucky enough to be a full time resident.

As I walk the beach now and find a piece of sea glass, I can feel my Dad walking beside me. I remember his words, "Once you get Long Beach Island sand between your toes, no other beach is ever good enough."

S.S.L.

SEA SHELLS

As you journey along the beach
you will see many different shells,
beautiful treasures from the sea.
You will connect with many, but will
only choose a few to carry with you.

THE LESSON

As you walk through life you will
meet many people. They are all
beautiful treasures. You will connect
with many, but will keep only a few.
These are your forever friends.

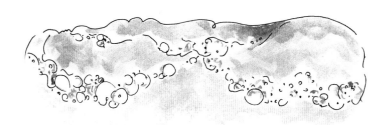

I feel the cold sand and water rushing between my toes. I can run into the huge tumbling waves. I am fearless, I am an Island Child. I can run into the ocean in February when it's cold as ice. I am an Island Child. I can run across the hot paved street without shoes on. I am an Island Child. I have the largest collection of sea shells and sea glass. I am an Island Child.   *L.O., age 12*

Sometimes when you're walking on the beach, you think you see a rare and valuable shell. But when you look at it closer and turn it around, it's not what you thought it was at all. A lesson I've learned is that you should pick your friends in life like you pick up shells on the beach. You can't just choose them because they're popular and look nice. You have to really look at the inside of their heart and see if they're nice to other people and nice to you. That's a genuine and valuable friend.   *D.R.O., age 9*

One of the lessons I learned from living on the Island is to never be afraid to be yourself. If you are boring and being someone you're not, no one is going to like you for who you are. It's just like the shell. If you find a shell that looks like every other shell, you wouldn't want to keep it. You would want a shell that is bold and different. I am different; I would never try to be like someone else. I am a shell like no other.   *C.B., age 12*

STARFISH

A marine animal with five arms stretching outward creating the shape of a STAR. The starfish is not really a fish even though it is called one. It does not have vertebrae or fins. It is actually a SEA STAR.

— THE LESSON —

There are two lessons from the Sea Star:

1. Do not let others define YOU. Define YOURSELF. Be who and what you want to be!
2. Live with open arms. A life led with open arms, open eyes and an open mind is a rich one.

When I walk along the shore of the Island I never tire of seeing myriad numbers of sea creatures—from the channeled whelk to the sand dollar to the thousands of colored shells deposited on the shoreline. I stop and look in awe and think of the long journey they took before these sea creatures arrived at the water's edge. The lesson I learn is to admire the beauty, the symmetry and the utter uniqueness of each of these small miracles of nature. On my walk I hope to be inspired to go deep within myself to create something of beauty so that I, too, may leave something behind in my creative journey—just like the ocean does every minute of every day, 365 days a year. And I hope my art will inspire others just as the Island continues to inspire me and attract people of all ages to come, look, listen and take in every aspect of its beauty.   *R.M., age 64*

I have lived on Long Beach Island my entire life. Here are a few of the many things I have learned:

1. How to walk barefoot over hot streets, sand, and stones.

2. While taking sharp turns on your bike, beware of sand patches.

3. Lick the sides of your ice cream cone at all times to keep it from melting!

4. Mini-golf is the best non-water island sport there is! (And it IS possible to get a hole-in-one on every hole across the Island)

5. You can find the best shells (and starfish!) after a good winter storm.

6. Some island secrets should be kept only with the locals!

7. Some of the best friends are your summer friends.

8. Embrace the off season — sometimes it is boring, but blinking yellow lights are the best!

9. Appreciate shoobies — Yes, they actually serve a purpose!

10. Long Beach Island is my home, and I never want to live anywhere else!   *K.G., age 23*

SUN

A star, a big ball of burning gas that provides heat and light for our solar system. It can do only one thing: SHINE. That one solitary thing creates all of our seasons and sustains life!

..—THE LESSON —..

Shine with all your might!
Just be you — that is enough.

70

I love the Island because it gives me the opportunity to really connect with my husband and my children in a way that is natural and relaxing — and stress free. I cherish our time together at the ocean. The best part of our day is when we sit on the beach—the sun is setting, the waves are breaking, the kids are playing and my husband and I are able to reflect on the day and imagine tomorrow.

N.M.B., age 48

The sight of the sunlight dancing on the water like a million diamonds sparkling hypnotizes my mind to a place of complete calm.

The sound of the rhythm of the waves lapping up to the beach is the lullaby that soothes all of my troubles.

The feel of the warmth of the sun from the top of my head, over every inch of my skin...down to my toes where the sand warms the soles of my feet is like a security blanket holding me tight.

With each breath I take, the taste of the salt in the air tantalizes my senses.

The smell of the ocean and the beach triggers a sense of peacefulness and pure serenity.

Standing, looking out over the vast ocean, renews my spirit and refreshes my perspective on life.

All of these are just a few of the sensual reminders that make me an Island Child.

J.L.G., age 40

As we need oxygen to fill our lungs and give us life, children of the Island consider the summer season a necessity to keep our hearts beating. The only thing that gets us through the bitter grey winter is the delight of the perfect summer ahead. Like a slowly approaching train whose destination leads you to the one you love, we anticipate the changing of seasons and arrival of summer solstice with open arms. Still shivering and frostbitten from the past winter, we are welcoming, and eager for the sun to come. We live to be free of rules and the dreary thoughts that control our minds until released by the salty ocean air as it soaks into our veins. We look forward to the new beginning that awaits us and count down the rise and set of infinite suns until the days stretch longer, the nights vibrate with excitement, and the sun begins to tan our pale longing skin. We get the satisfaction we've craved, like that of the ocean caressing the shoreline, knowing it will never be asked to linger long.

C.B., age 17

I am an Island Child because I have lived on the Island my whole life and I take advantage of all it has to offer. I swim like a fish and sail with the breeze. I appreciate waking up in the morning and watching the sun rise, smelling the fresh salt air, and listening to the sea gulls drop crabs and clamshells on our roof! It is like a vacation when you can go to the beach, sail and swim everyday!I love living on the island. My sister and I are very lucky Island Children. The island has a variety of fun things to do!

H.S., age 10 and H.S., age 7

A long car ride is a small price to pay when I'm heading straight to paradise. Memories and images fill my mind as I wait impatiently. The bright sun beams down on my tanned arms; an indescribable warmth immediately engulfs me. The refreshing ocean air is cool against my skin, whipping my brown locks around for that perfect summer look. Birds chirp songs in harmony, waves crash and move along endlessly. The second I see the sign, I let out a sigh of relief. My eyes scan

words I've memorized over and over again— "Welcome to Long
Beach Island." I'm home.   *D.D., age 16*

    The Jersey shore is my summer getaway. The bay is quiet as a mouse
until the squeaking sound of the seagulls and the T-Rex roar of the
rumbling motorboats send peaceful, hurtling waves over the bay. The
smiling sun and cotton ball clouds fill the sky. The sun beating down on
my back makes me look out and see the glancing shadows of the boats
and the small house in the distance. The slimy, slippery and fishy smell
catches my nose. The whoosh sound guides my ear into the bay. The
motion of the fishing line swaying back and forth is relaxing. Somehow
I feel that this is where I belong.

                                                        M.S., age 10

    In my 9 years as an Island Child, I've learned some "do's" and
"don'ts".
    1.Don't walk barefoot on the hot street in the summer.
    2.Do remain calm if a crab jumps out of the pot while your
grandmother is cooking it. Grab a net!
    3.Don't forget sunscreen... ouch.
    4.Do watch out for seagulls. You never when they are going to
have target practice!
    5.Don't freak out if you feel something on your leg in the ocean.
It was probably just a little fish, not a shark.
    6.Do hang on to the raft really tight when you are being pulled
by a boat. You never know when your Dad might turn hard...
    7.Don't swing your club too hard when playing mini-golf. You
might hit your cousin. hee hee.
    8.Do get a large ice cream, they don't melt as fast as a small.
    9..Do go to the beach at night. The moon lights up the waves.
It's electric.
    10.Don't worry about the smell coming over the bridge, it's just
low tide! Really!   *A.G.R., 9*

SURFING

Sit on the sand and watch some surfers.
Watch how many times they fall, miss
the wave and fight with strength and
determination to stay on the board. It
is a combination of their skill, timing
and perserverance that allows them
to experience the exhilaration of
riding a wave.

⸺ THE LESSON ⸺

Do not be afraid to fail.
Perservering through failure is how to
catch the perfect wave to success.
Falling is not failing.

I am an Island Child because I have lived here my whole life. Long Beach Island is my adventure, in the summer and winter! I love going to the beach in the summer and playing in the snow in the winter. I love to surf, kite board, and stand up paddle in the summer!

In the winter and summer I love to help my mom and dad in our family surf shop. It is called Island Surf and Sail. I love going to school on the Island in the winter because all of my friends go to school with me. It is quiet on the Island in the winter. Long Beach Island is a WONDERFUL place! I could not imagine the world without Long Beach Island!

Z.D., age 10

I've lived on this island my whole life! The scariest thing I learned was when I drifted in the deep. I thought I was good at boogie-boarding, so I went farther out where the big kids go. I was too small to paddle back so I was going farther and farther out and I was very scared. My Mom got the lifeguards to help and I was close to fainting. I got out and I was miserable! I finally know that if you want to go far look at the flags, or good luck!

O.T., age 11

I am an Island Child because I'm always near the water. Whether I'm surfing, boogie boarding, or swimming, I can't stay away from the water. Almost every day I go for a walk on the beach. A lot of the time when it's too cold to surf, I just lie down and watch the waves.

S.T.Y., age 11

I love the Island because I can skim and crash into the waves. I have learned never to skim board into 30-foot waves.

L.V.L., age 7

TIDES

Tides are the rise and fall of the water on earth. High and low tides are caused by the gravitational forces between the earth, the moon and sun. Gravity itself is not visable, but its effect on the entire planet is clearly visable as we watch the tides change.

— THE LESSON —

Your surroundings have a profound effect on you, even the things you cannot see.

I am an Island Child. To me, the smell of low tide is oddly comforting. Walking over hot sand is easier barefoot. And Ice cream sandwiches taste even better with a little sand mixed in.

I.H., age 34

My high school graduation quote was "being yourself should be as natural and constant as the rhythm of the ocean".

A.C.A.

My two cousins loved to fish. They also lived two blocks away. So much of my childhood life on Long Beach Island revolved around chasing those two boys as they chased fish. They still chase fish today. I can't' say I loved fishing back then' in fact I really didn't care for it at all. But where they went I went too. And although I never imagined my adulthood would still revolve around the thrill of a day's catch, I seem to always reflect back on those carefree days, growing up fishing on Long Beach Island.

The waters of Long Beach Island were our playground. We fished, swam and crabbed our way through our childhood, moving from ocean to bay with the same ease and reliability as the evening tide. You would think that I, the tag-along girl cousin, would have loved to fish, but nothing could have been further from the truth. Casting a reel or baiting a line was not something I did often. While they threw cast after cast, I would draw hearts in the sand and collect shells and skate egg sacs. The love of fishing never really bit me but I can still remember their excited faces when the methodic tug of the line suddenly tugged back.

A.M.R.

The beauty of the ocean, the brilliance of the sun, the laughter of children, so much FUN. My daughter worked at The Island Shop when she was fifteen through twenty-one years old. One dreadful storm was quite frightening when we received a call that we needed to pick her up, as the water was flooding in from the ocean and the bay. In the middle of this water was the Island Shop, a lovely clothing store. Quickly we ran to pick up our sixteen-year-old daughter to bring her home to the mainland, to safety. Do not underestimate the strength of a storm.

M.M., age 56

I am an Island Child because I have lived here. I have seen the best and worst this island is capable of. I have lived through its horrible storms and its big flooding. The Island has good and bad things, delights and horrors. I have seen them because I am an Island Child.

E.Y., age 12

Long Beach Island is my favorite place to kayak and catch baby eels and terrapins. *E.S., age 7*

I am an Island Child because I like splashing around in the waves, going boogie boarding with my cousin, Ava. I love to ride on the tube in the back of the boat or go crabbing or fishing. It's also really fun to go in the tide pools on the beach. There is always something interesting to see in them. Other than being at the beach or on the bay, my favorite activity to do is to walk to buy a delicious book and to have mint-chocolate-chip ice cream. That would be a perfect LBI day.

C.E.P., age 9

Spending each summer down Long Beach Island, I got to know the rhythms of the ocean, the wind, the waves. I had a large family and had to carve out time alone; I loved the time after five at night, on the beach. The lifeguards and bathers were gone, the seagulls were coming out, I knew it was hectic at home, and that mom would send Rich, my baby brother, down to get me, just minutes before the dinner would go

78

on the table. She knew I needed this time.

I felt neither "here nor there" because the rush of summer was over, a few friends I had made had gone back to the city, and I was anticipating school and yet not really looking forward to it either.

I sat in the surf; you could only do this when the tide was low and gentle, and let the water flow over me. I remember the water was lighter and paler blue than it had been all summer, almost clear as it went over my head. It truly looked like a liquid aquamarine. The nights were getting shorter, the breezes a little cooler, but only at night as the sun went down. I was restless, and being here calmed me so. I remember I was nine years old.

L.P., age 67

What I most like about the Island is its beach because you can easily fall asleep listening to the waves.

H.S., age 12

I am an Island Child because I couldn't imagine a better place to begin and end each day. Falling deeply asleep to the sounds of the rumbling surf and hum of crickets and awaking each morning to the sun and mellow tide is my definition of perfection.

M.H., age 28

The air on a summer LBI day is salted with undercurrents of … joy, that's just what it is. Catch it swelling in and out of earshot … kids squealing at the washing waves … imploring for ice cream (the jangle of the treat truck's bell is stronger than the tide)… at dinner, the clank of glasses from the rooftop deck, toasting a good day. Here's to more! As sure as the sun kisses here first.

M.S.

A WALK ON THE BEACH

Walking on a beach allows you to experience nature and each other. To see the many stages of life, watch the beach walkers go by:

Parents tightly holding the hand of a small child by the water's edge. An adult walks alone, reflecting on her thoughts and sees only the waves, the sand, the shells... A couple holding hands, experiencing the beauty together as if it is just the two of them alone on the beach... Friends walking closely in sync, chatting as they lose themselves in conversation... A grandparent walks at the same slow pace as the grandchild, explaining all they see together.

—— THE LESSON ——

Treasure the talk, treasure the walk, treasure the journey.

I'm an Island Child because the ocean is the same color as my eyes and my hair has gold in it like the sand. We look alike so, we are kind of like related. I love living on the island near the beach, but I wish my bed was on the sand right next to the ocean. The seagulls could sleep on my pillow and my sheets would be full of sand and shells, but no seaweed. That would be gross. I could look at the ocean all day, it makes me really happy. The ocean helps me to be a good bodysurfer. I like swimming in the bay and watching my sister stick black snails all over her arms. I can't pick a favorite part of the island that I love the best. I love it all and I know it loves me back.

J.R.R., age 7

As a young girl, I fell in love with the Island. I love it more as I get older. While vacationing, I met my husband 48 years ago. The Island has given me more than I could have ever imagined as I walked the beach as a young girl...four beautiful children, six darling grandchildren who share the love of the Island also. I am thankful for the Island and the love, memories and happiness it has given to me.

B.E.G., age 66

I have always been an Island Child. I have felt at home on the Island since becoming a part of it at age eleven. Each and every trip to the Island is a coming home for me; the air, the calm, the people, the feeling, the peace... all the things that make it such a special and magical place. My dreams are to live there, to breathe there, to raise my children there, and to forever call home there. And no matter if I live all or only some of my days there, I will always be an Island Child.

M.S.C., age 31

81

Beach Walk and Baby Shells:

I walk the beach today at a slower pace in the dry sand.
I take my time looking for shells.
I used to rush to cover distance while enjoying the lovely views and thinking.
Today I use all of my sense to take in the beauty of the beach.
My sense of sight is delighted with the deep hues of the water along with the white foam.
My sense of smell is filled with the salt air mixed with suntan lotion.
My sense of hearing is constantly picking up the sounds of conversations, music, squealing children blending with the pounding surf.My sense of touch is the feeling of soft warm sand between my toes and the warmth of the sun on my skin.
With all of thes are the memories…
In my mind and heart are the days of holding a small hand and jumping over waves.
Little sandy feet that needed help and support to walk in the sand.
There is this lovely flash to a different time when the lace bonnet showed wisps of bleached blond baby fine hair blowing in the gentle summer breeze.
Everything in life was perfect.
Have things changed?
Most things are as they always were and will always be at the beach.
But the little hand does not reach up for support.
The little feet are steady and strong and walk with grace, beauty and confidence.
The past is a lovely, beautiful, happy memory.
The baby shells remind me of you.
Yes, the beach is the same.
And life is perfect-different but perfect-
It is just as it should be.
I walk slower.
I take more time to enjoy.
I bend down to pick up baby shells.
I celebrate you.
The little girl who grew up to become the beautiful woman who is my daughter.

C.K.

Que Dios te Bendiga

Blest is this salty Island Child
Each so wet and oh so wild.
Intaglio shapes of wind and water,
Elements create son and daughter
A sun-lit face with sun-kissed skin,
Bedazzled in bronze; our next-of-kin.
Nonchalant and naturally... in bare feet,
Ready to rollick within tide's beat.
Cultivars of perpetual motion,
individuals sporting love for the ocean
Anchored right here, C'est la vie:
To an Island Child, there is only the sea.

B.A.

SEA FOG

A form of fog created when warm moist air over the ocean moves across the cool surface of the land. Only wind can dissipate this fog.

·— THE LESSON —·

We all have days when nothing appears clear. Don't make decisions based on what you think you see; make them based on what you know.

Afterword

I am an Island Child only by chance. All of life is chance, of course, and the circumstances that deposited my footprints here were no more planned than the effects of a northeast storm rearranging sand on the beach.

So, fittingly, it was during a March storm that I crossed over the causeway bridge for the first time. I was not so much a child as a late-adolescent, joining friends on a fledgling weekly newspaper here. It had been a long drive and I walked in darkness to the 28th Street beach in Ship Bottom, wanting to sense the change in geography, thrilled to hear (and feel) the waves rolling in. I listened to the ocean that first night through clapboard walls of a '50s beach house long-since updated, and the memories carry with them the smell of that musty house, as comfortable as a pair of old, well-worn boat shoes. (It's the kind of affection that time offers.)

And yet my first daylight impression of Long Beach Island was, to be frank, not enchanting. All those crowded houses! Raised ranches — not a whole lot of character here… endless telephone poles and wires! Where was the open space? You call those dunes? It was grey, cold, and damp, as March at the beach often is. My early beach experiences had been on Cape Cod and freshwater lakes inland, and I wasn't so sure about this New Jersey shore thing!

But I became enlightened, shall we say, and even the nondescript raised ranches and the Boulevard-length views of utility poles and blinking off-season lights eventually grew on me. I had only planned to spend a spring and summer here, but stayed a winter, then a year, and then a few decades. I think I was hooked that first winter, 1977-78, when the Island was desolate and a terrible blizzard shut down the state. I almost sailed from my Loveladies lagoon winter rental ($150 a month!) down the icy, drifted-over boulevard to friends at the south end of Harvey Cedars; I trudged to the beach to see the ocean chewing away at the dunes, long creaming waves retreating and roaring up again and again. I felt the sting of sand and snow pelting my face in the gale. I loved it. This was the ancient, eternal Island, the forces of nature acting as they had for millennia. I felt both insignificant and very much alive.

It is the Island Child within that has allowed me to recognize that change is a constant. Just as a barrier island is created by shifting, changing natural forces, so must we. I welcome the changes, and the moments delivered by island chance. I dove in head first.

It was, after all, an Island Child's chance that had me living from one end of the Island to the other, from the oceanside to the bayside, from a old Victorian in Beach Haven (still with its 19th century dust) to the "suburbs" of High Bar Harbor, from a solid hundred-year-old Lifesaving Service house to a classic old oceanfront nestled in the dunes. I put my roots down for a while in a shotgun-style houseboat (with undulating floors) that had been dragged onto the meadows and stayed put as new construction went up around it. It was Island chance that led me to my first friends here who lived in the iconic shack on the causeway, the scene of a few wild parties; later I was the last "tenant;" when a wall collapsed as we nailed new sheathing on the roof, we had second thoughts about that rental. Chance then led me to live in what once had been Kinsey's General Store in Harvey Cedars that summer, where we sat on the old porch and watched thunderstorms roll in from the west, or the endless entertainment at the Exxon station across the street.

Today my home is on what was once a forgotten, overlooked road through salt marsh to the bay, opposite the Island; when the old clam house was sold to me, the clammer said, "don't be a stranger" and toasted the deal, not with a drink, but with a few clams he opened at his roadside farm stand.

And over the years, this island, this shore, has shared so much more with me — great friendships, experiences, an Island Child wife and son. I've experienced moments of humility, of good fortune, of privilege, trouble and foolishness, friendship and love, and the Island Child's insight to realize how rare and precious such gifts can be.

Ray Fisk

Island Child Contributors

(In order of appearance)

Dylan Cecchini
Liam Moran
Chase Bradley
Dawn Little Kennedy
Paige Thompson Caistro
Alexis K. Lally
Robert M. Gray, Jr.
Rose Delfico
Susan Kramer
Nancey J. Cameron
Jeanette Levy
Linda D. Okupski
Katie Powers
Thais McAleece Haines
Debbie Adamo
Leslie T. Engelhart
Kathy Hefferle
Victoria G. Palmer
Sharon L. Girgenti
Jonathan A. Gray
Margaret Thomas Buchholz
Danny Arnone
Diane McTigue
Eric Houghton
Emily Micciche
Carol Freas
Fiona Foster
Walter J. Moss
Daniel Dunlap
Jonathan Dunlap
Johnny Tilton
Avila S. Reynolds
Timothy Brindley
Landon Childs
Natalie Aftanis
Diane Stulga
J. Hughes
J. Loftus
Liam Sullivan
Lori Wisnieski
Griffen Arnone
Sandy Gingras
Debbie Coughlin
Britin Miller
Eileen Hessel
Charles Kraemer
Annie Larkin
Gabrielle A. Cabaron

Elle Cecchini
Amanda R. McClellan
Jody Davis
Andrea Cavallaro Lynch
Linda A. Queiroz
Bryan Kahl
Karen D. Whitaker
Frank T. Palermo
Dena Musantry
Sean Kahl
Wendy S. Magnan
Bryce C. Reynolds
Susanne Kotch
Mary McGuinty
Denise P. Green
Jessica M. Hammond
Cayla Casler
Franny Andahazy
J.S
Pamela Gray
Beth G. Pagan
Dillion Van Liew
Kayla Lynch
Danielle DiSomma
Aylin Miranda
Laura T. Patterson
Madi Green
Clare McCarthy
Liam Sheward
Darlene Kowalski
Jennifer Oetzel
Lucas Micciche
Luke Yates
Anna Zalepa
Sharon Ogburn
Kelly Fontana
Teagan Cunningham
Sam Boardman
Whitney Ransome
Debbie Dooling
Kathy Sheward
Laurie VanSant
Patricia T. Espenak
Leslee Ganss
Kathy Devitt
Caitlin E. Gioe
Carole Bradshaw
Diane L. Entrikin

Benjamin W. Palmer
Beth G. Pagan
Grace Nedeau
Amanda Sheward
Aaron N. Palmer
Bridget Marshall
Tara Williamson
Susan Pence
Mary Lee Pence
Veronica Grace-Marie Ruoff
Maura L. Flynn
Olivia Lattanzi
Mellisa Micciche
Kelly Miller
Sandi Smith-Lusk
Elizabeth O'Hara
Devon R.Oetzel
Chase Bendik
Regina Montana
Kelsey Goddard
Nancy Butler
Jodi L. Girgenti
Coral Baugh
Hannah Skimmons
Haley Skimmons
Dani Duke
Megan Shokoff
Ava G. Ruff
Zoe Deakyne
Olivia Tilton
Tyde Yakelewicz
Logan Van Liew
Irene Hughes
Annice M. Rainone
Mary McGrath
Ethan Yates
Elizabeth Swan
Caroline E. Palmer
Lyn Procopio
Hugo Sanchez
Mollie Hartman
Maria Scandale
Jackson R. Ruff
Barbara E. Gray
Megan S. Corsi
Carol Krom
Bianca Aniski

Other contributors not in the book can be found on www.theislandchild.com

87

Life Lessons by Corinne G. Ruff

Born in Trenton, N.J., the second of four children, Corinne Gray Ruff grew up on the sugar sand beaches of L.B.I. and Manahawkin. She attended the Florida Institute of Technology where she pursued her dream of becoming an airline pilot. She flew as a flight instructor, fish spotter pilot, corporate pilot and currently flies for a commercial airline domestically and internationally on the Boeing 757 and 767.

Her family history on Long Beach Island dates back to the 1930s; her parents met on 16th Street in Surf City 46 years ago. She lives in Surf City with her husband Mark, also a pilot, and their two Island Children, Ava and Jackson.

Illustrations by Lisa M. Benjamin

Lisa M. Benjamin's earliest works were etched along the sandy shores of New Jersey, where she was born and raised. She is a working artist and educator, having the pleasure of teaching visual arts to Island Children on Long Beach Island for over 20 years. Lisa lives in Forked River, N.J. with her husband Charles and their son Zachary.

Down The Shore Publishing
*specializes in books, calendars, videos and cards about Long Beach Island
and the Jersey Shore. For a free catalog of all our titles
or to be included on our mailing list, just send us a request:*

email: dtsbooks@comcast.net

Down The Shore Publishing
P.O. Box 100 • West Creek, NJ 08092

www.down-the-shore.com